Cutlish

Also by Rajiv Mohabir

Poetry:

The Taxidermist's Cut

The Cowherd's Son

Nonfiction:

Antiman: A Hybrid Memoir

Translation:

I Even Regret Night: Holi Songs of Demerara by Lalbihari Sharma

Cutlish

Rajiv Mohabir

For crossers of land, sky, rivers, sea.
For crossers of flame.
For all queers and antiman kind—

Library of Congress Cataloging-in-Publication Data

Names: Mohabir, Rajiv, author.
Title: Cutlish / Rajiv Mohabir.
Description: First edition. | New York : Four Way Books, [2021] |
Identifiers: LCCN 2021005286 | ISBN 9781945588884 (paperback)
Subjects: LCGFT: Poetry.
Classification: LCC PS3613.O376 C88 2021 | DDC 811/.6--dc23

This book is manufactured in the United States of America and printed on
acid-free paper.

Four Way Books is a not-for-profit literary press. We are grateful for the assistance
we receive from individual donors, public arts agencies, and private foundations.

This publication is made possible with public funds from the
National Endowment for the Arts

and from the New York State Council on the Arts, a state agency,

We are a proud member of the Community of Literary Magazines and Presses.

Contents

अ आ इ ई उ ऊ

ए ऐ ओ औ ऋ

क ख ग घ ङ

च छ ज झ ञ

ट ठ ड ढ ण

त थ द ध न

प फ ब भ म

य र ल व

श ष स ह

cut·lish /ˈkət·lIʃ/ *noun*

1.   *cutlass,*

2.   British blade, machete,

3.   colony blister of cane knife—

4.   Demerara-brown sugar

5.   kidneys, toes, eyes,

6.

7.   El Dorado rum rot—

Bhagwati, my Aji, opens a cream soda bottle top with her teeth. She pours it into a glass and mixes it with tinned milk. *Langtime, dis whole place been bush, all about. Abi tek a-cutlish an clean 'am.* Her ordhni slips from her head.

The Po-Co Kid

maatahet logan bol na sake hai
darsana nahin maral, murjhaake

Let's get one thing queer—I'm no Sabu-like sidekick,
I'm the main drag. Ram Ram in a sari; salaam

on the street. I don't speak Hindu, Paki, or Indian,
can't control minds, have no psychic powers.

I clip my yellow nails at dusk; on Saturday nights
I shave my head. Forgive me Shiva,

forgive me Saturn. I'm Coolie on Liberty Ave, desi
in Jackson Heights—where lights spell *Seasons Greetings*

to cover Christmas, Diwali, and Eid—
where white folks in ethnic aisles ask, *Will your parents*

arrange your bride? while Ma and I scope out fags,
gyaff, and laugh while aunties thread our eyebrows.

> *"The subaltern cannot speak.*
> *Representation has not withered away."*

Indo-Queer I

toke oise naam gandu aur faggot *de deila*
toke Paki *aur* antiman *pukarela*

Mehndi marks on your palms betray your body
as do the jaggery ducts of your palate.

The night you tear into the world, the pandit
opens his book to line your spine with stars.

Yuh limin' sunburned sting of salt and silk,
those pretty-boys cyan't take yuh peppah,

can't tread the Caribbean brine, wild and wide,
in your tongue, can't mend the cutlass gash of your eyes.

Before Empire's letters spelled out *homo*
you tied saris and danced launda ke naach.

Now the white Christian wants to bind you down
in his cellar, horny to tear your throat open.

> *They give the name ass-fuck, faggot.*
> *They call you these things: Paki and antiman.*

Dove (or Tell Me the Number of Your Plane)

ordhni ke torde, hamar jiyara tardpela
tohar tir jaisan najariya: jaherila

A scorpion stings me, its toxins swim my veins,
one ill prick from you and I writhe in your fever.

I dream I cough up a songbird I release to the sky,
you board a plane to take you across the desert.

I will tie messages to the feet of doves,
set them to sail at dusk with a map to your country.

Dizzy with thirst they fall, raining, from high,
dried meat hardening under tawny feathers.

I throw stones at planes' shadows, cursing iron
to crash, to burn in serrated-leafed cane fields.

So my skin never blisters with your desire,
in birdbaths I empty vials of avicide.

My veil torn, I shake and quiver,
your eyes: poisonous arrows.

Sapera, the Snake Charmer

jamin ke mati ke niche, ka sutal hai
hirde ke jardwa mein kaun uljhaal hai

What is January's ice if not starling ghosts
on the park's oaks? A cloud of star-breasted feathers

lifts skyward. Your curse, a skilled tar-tongued tune
whose frost I cannot stop my ears from heeding.

My skin scales over with copper coins. You rest
my red coils in your bamboo basket and pick

my nickels off one by one. My captor-love,
I once relied on our heat. No need to knock my teeth—

The cobra who eats dead meat for months, runs dry
of venom. O Sapera, your flute, a dousing rod

bereft of bird-psalm, stokes thirst in my woven
tokri and I'm unable to strike your reed or heel.

What sleeps under the earth;
what entangles itself amongst the heart's roots?

Falling from a Plane

brahma tu julum bhaile, piya dur na bhejo
hamar paache chale na koi, hamar sahej na jai

When I am ashy and parched, whose palms will whet me,
will slice the clouds with a knife of gold or glass?

The day we meet you board a plane to Toronto.
Give me water, my tongue thick with pennies

in the Meat Packing district on the Hudson, please—
come fuck me. But on my back you place a cobra.

I set oblations adrift in my blood of cane flowers,
until I am the Kaieteur river cascade.

Rushing his rocks, gouging a ravine below,
I maelstrom ice cubes with a straw in my scotch.

Always across from the wrong man at the bar,
I smile sin wide, invited into his bed.

Brahma, you tyrant! Do not call my love away,
No one walks behind me, I have no peace.

Lordha and Sil

ghare hindi na bole jaila ta ka baat hai
chattaan pe rassi ragarde se chaap rehejai

I buy a flat stone to carry on the plane;
the TSA agent makes me explain what once ground

household spices now languishes, a curio
of ancestral time: bondage and a release

of readapted tongues. I've flattened my fingers
milling cumin, pise all kine masala.

What is a mortar without a pestle, a Guyanese
without pepper sauce or chutney; exile without

a home to throw a prince from; a stone without
salt-grooves of brown and turmeric hands that marked it,

the savor of indenture in every pounded garlic
clove, an epic voyage rendered new in English?

So what if in the home we don't speak Hindi?
A rope rubbing against a rock leaves an imprint.

Curry Powder

curry powder *se bani tarkariya*
masala pise na jane, na jane

Nani's mother forgot her first Madrasi name;
adopted by Christians off the indenture ship

called jahaj. Nani ground garam masala with
bitter bitter tears so Ma buys Lala's from the West

Indies Mart and parrots, *Achha hai?* to her elders.
My sister pops a sachet of Trader's premade lentils

and shakes each grain into Nana's karahi.
My brother can't distinguish barah from phulowri

though Ma fries both from grine-daal. He eats all two,
wet with plenty plenty pepper sauce, come morning

he rass go burn. I make rice in a steamer that plugs
into the wall, its final ding calls us all to feast.

Curry becomes curry with curry powder,
I do not know how to grind masala.

11

Hassa

After Aja drowned
and piranhas picked his body, Aji
went to the trench with a stick
and disturbed the fish's nest
so they leapt from the water
straight into her basket, as
she sucked her teeth and laughed
to herself *'E go eat sweet,*
but I live seas away,
so Ma freezes her pan for me
after blood of lung and gas-
bladder spread red
across her butcher-block
in her attempt to recreate Aji's specialty—
Ma knows exactly where
on the belly, between the head
and plates to insert her ceramic knife,
to cut down and to push
her fingers into the macabre
cavity and rip from
the meat gall, pancreas,
the Miocene lung-type vessels
and Ma's heart chamber opened
despite its rusted latch,

she still plays Anuradha Paudwal's
cham-cham-chamke chandani
in the trench of this Floridian kitchen
where I slip my fingernail
underneath one plate
close to the base of the tail
and pull it forward
so all the non-scales stack
exposing orange flesh,
I look for the egg sack,
whitish and curry but find,
instead, in the hassa's mouth
a silver coin sparkle like
four drachma in the canal
to pay the temple tax,
but the real miracle
Aji clung to, a secret
Ma knows also, is this catfish
called *hassar* before
in Guyanese we dropped
the "r" to *hassa* stewed in pumpkin
in Hindustani means *laugh*
and that Aji and Ma
have been laughing this whole time

and that this laughing fish
is the avatar of the shekel parable,
and that Aji and Ma
like disciples of survival,
without knowing where,
threw lines in the lake
and trusted enough to live
without men in their nests.

अ ā इ ई उ ऊ

ए ऐ ओ औ ऋ

क ख ग घ ङ

cha छ ज झ ञ

ट ठ ड ढ ण

त थ द ध न

प फ ब भ ma

य र ल व

श ष sa ह

Angreji Ke Sarap

Dark Goddess of me, ii sab puri hoijai.
My eyes kajal-streaked, red each jewel-seed take root—
I yank out my uvula to tithe. suno.
May each face who ever said, *Speak English*
find their own tongue fettered and split,
my mixed blood hardening their faces.
May this dialect of guns poison the mouths
of those who dehumanize the bound, who have ever
called me *Coolie crabdog*. Ma, I curse this spider-speech
of dacoits and brigands with the power
of seven seas, the voice of the hurricane,
the razor of cane leaves to rot into soil that brings
the sprouts of my mother patois into leaf.
okar raaj khatam hoijai, me sarape you skunt.

English forgets the fields it clears.

Put into ecological terms, it's an invasive species choking out the
      native plants and birds.

A crabdog is a real animal, imagine my surprise: Crab-eating fox.
      Forest fox. Maikong. *Cerdocyon thous.* Not a true fox, of course.

Sometimes my tongue tastes sharp like metal and a canine tooth.

Creole is not a true language, of course.

For this, I curse English—the language that sows silence.

hamar aji angreji nahi bol sake rahe, uu khali aisan baat bol sake
    rahe, sab mix-mix karke.

suno, uu jab bachchi rahe okar mai-bap ke khali hindustani ke soch rahe.

uu ka jaane ki ek-go din aapan betiya ke potwa ii murjhaal perd ke
    pani chardhe jai.

saphal hoi ke na—kaun jani?

uu ka jaan sake rahe ki okar santaan angrej deswa me se langtime ke
    jhanda utaijai.

English bulldozes old growth. Hindustani is a ghost in my mouth.

What accent do you hear in my voice? How about now?

How about now?

Now?

NAMA-stay in yoga pants, OM tattoos, *mera naam Rita-Christina hai.*

The white girl whose parents own a three-story home in Westchester
     practices yoga and now at the Diwali Mela wears a sari.

She's been studying Hindi and loves when Indians congratulate
     her grammar.

I just love your culture. The American government pays people like
     her to learn about people like you.

Rita-Christina is allowed to vacation in your skin.

When Aji sang Hindustani songs, missionaries filled her mouth
     with coals.

Tongueless, what could she pass down to her fledglings already
     quoting Wordsworth?

My mother in a sari? White women already overlook her for promotion.

Even when she speaks English no one hears English.

Household Phrases:

a. *Aji only speaks broken English*

b. *But the British gave us so much, do you still want to be poor
in India?*

c. *That's not real Hindi. It's broken. tutal bhail.*

d. *...Coolie crabdog...*

e. *Na talk so outside, de English man go undastan'?*

f. *Abi-dis broken people*

g. *Why you wan' learn fe talk Hindustani talk—
fahget dis madness*

After Aji died I could speak her language to no one.

English is silence where once we taan-sang.

They believed her tongue broken and like some dark spell it broke
off, a trident splinter in my mouth.

I tie a bundle with disappearance: a compact at birth.

Talk straight, Coolie-witch, let me hear.

I open my mouth and scorpions shimmer out.

:::obeah to unbreak a tongue:::

In wet beach sand cut *tutal,*

                    broken with a cutlass.

Watch the waves reclaim,

                    rejoin, *aapnaye, phir se jorde—*

tohar muh se ek-go phul girela/

kabita pardhe khatir uu toke Congress ke Library mein bulawela/

yaso ek jagah tohar khatir bati, uuhi jagah kabitiya bati/

kitne bar Magistrate tohar crabdog jubaan mana kare rahe/

tu ab rakshas ke jigardwa mein rahela, angrej bhojan karela, angrej
        manus ke chudela/

tohar jubaan ujar tara bati, ek-go chameli jeke alabama mein
        konfejrat jazmin bole jaila/

aisan kabitan likho jaun sablogan samajh sakelan, sab farren
        batiya nikaalo/

hiya uu logan aapan ke tantra-mantra ke pustak rakhe bati je
        batiyawe ke-ke ameriki hoi sakela/

tu manch par awela aja-aji, nana-nani ke bhasiya bolat/

je tohar andar nikal urde lagela aur vaha sabhilogan ke sange tohar
        aji-aja, nana-nani *wah wah* bolat baital rahe/

ii pahile samay ke capital mein ek-go Coolie bolal hai/

ka tu uuhi pahile Coolie bati je tutal hoike bolela/

kahin tutal cheej dekhal jaila/

/a flower falls from your mouth

/they call you to the Library of Congress to read a poem

/there is a place for you, that place is poetry

/how many times did White-samaj make your crabdog talk illegal

/you now live in the heart of Empire, eat White food, fuck a White man

/your tongue is a white star, called a confederate jasmine in Alabama

/write poems that everyone can relate to, take out these foreign words and phrases

/in this place they keep their sacred knowledge of who gets to be American

/you approach the podium and begin to speak your Aja-Aji, Nana-Nani's language

/something inside of you breaks and there in the audience your Aja-Aji,
Nana-Nani are sitting, *wah wah*s on their hands and lips

/was this the first time a Coolie spoke in the capital

/are you the first Coolie to speak your broken self

/do you still see anything that's broken

अ ā इ ई उ ऊ

ए ऐ ओ औ ऋ

क ख ga घ ङ

cha छ ज झ ञ

ट ठ ड ढ -

त थ द dha न

प फ ब भ ma

य र ल व

श ष sa ह

Beta, me Aja come from India. When me Aja an' Aji left Kalkota fe come a-Guyana, me Aji been a-pregnant an' me papa born in de ship. You know langtime you come in a-boat name jahaj—de same big big ship wha' come from India. De does call matti jahaji—de people wha' come from de boat. Dis side ke people, de English, de white man from dis side say, 'Leh abi go Guyana,' *or* 'Abi go Trinidad, or anywhere da side. You know, a-you get job an' a-you go de good. An' one-two year aftah a-you go come back.'

Coolie

Coolie *naam dharaiya je hamke tej pakardaye*
cutlish jaisan kate hamke Guyanwa *mein aaike*

With this whip-scar iron shackle name Aja
contract-bound, whole day cut cane; come night he drink

up rum for so until he wine-up and pitch in
the trench's black water and cries, *Oh Manager!*

until sugar and pressure claim he two eyes.
De backra manager laugh we—so come so done.

I was born a crabdog devotee of the silent
god, the jungle god, the god crosser-of-seas. White tongues

licked the sweet Demerara of my sores. Now
Stateside, Americans erase my serf story;

call me *Indian*. Can't they hear kalapani
in my voice, my breath's marine layer when I say?

> *They made us hold the name* Coolie,
> *like a cutlass it bit us coming to Guyana.*

Hiranyagarbha

Born of cane stalk I am
      the first mad(wo)man to descend
barrack steps into a body

      of petals. In some Indian story
this grass is my ancestor,
      but I don't know it. To forget

means to survive; I am expert
      at amnesia, new-moon faced,
I have my own mantra. Somewhere

      my navel string sleeps
under handfuls of rice-field dirt
      my father's father threw

into sky, to forecast gravity
      of shaping a ship or a pile
of shit. Now the land is erased

      under my feet. I am told
I am nameless, we've spit out
      English, but this game

of interpreting shadow,
      reading bodies into holes
of text: a memory trick of presence.

      O Ancestors, I've inherited passing:
how to disappear straight and
      to alveolarize my name, all blue,

bribed by silk and hate, a relic:
      a lover's lip, a dead queer's tongue
that licks assholes bald,

      back against shipboards,
the many toothed snake
      striking this body: a well

terrible with kalapani.

Kalapani

means water's black
means sea crossers, means
to forget secrets and rituals, means
conversion, means cloud cover,
means night means
sunset, means loss, means
water in the breath,
means to mislay
your name, means orphaning,
means taking the name
Coolie, means breaking
under bundles of cane stalk,
means Guyana, means
migration, means America, means
voyage, means to remain
living, means planting
seeds in your ancestors' sweat,
means salt and sea-
change, means a story's new
lea, means a yield
of fruit, means
to generate, means
to rise as the sun

Snowfall in the Tropics

ham uu badariya jaise bhatak rahe, akela
jaun pahar aur ghatiya ke upar urdela

On every corner a festival of white dis side.
Outside the rain of jasmine or ash—

snow drifts. Snow swallows the earth whole.
Snow first, then the namaste of daffodil heads

breach the ice mirror. Their buried bones
gleam silver, deep within earth skins, old poems

figure-skate their palates, carving X marks into thumbs.
They're glad for the frost, turmeric lips bow to the ground.

They spell their names in an ever-pallid garland of Xs,
outside their homes rain jasmine or ash—

It's Christmas and *I'm dreaming of a* white *Christmas*.
It's Christmas and they call small bananas figs.

> *"I wandered lonely as a cloud*
> *That floats on high o'er vales and hills…"*

Offering

jab mathiya hamar ban jai, ta ham chalab
ham na aaib, but ham na jani ki uu mar jai

The pandit flutters tantra-mantras in Sanskrit
and deep Hindi, chirped only by the people who

stretch asanas in midtown on measured lunch
breaks. In the land of erasure, I rum myself clean,

touch my lips to the bottle as I drink; think
Pitripaksh means the wings of the ancestors—

the fortnight to offer the forefathers kush grass.
From its torso I pull a peppershrike's entrails,

damn myself twice in English, a dwijah,
a bananaquit's blood in my nail beds. Hear Aji,

None na de fe charawe. Here there's no such son,
I worship foremothers. I eat the bird's wild heart.

> *"When my temple is built, then I will come.*
> *If I will not come, I will not know if he is dead."*

37

South Asian Art Exhibit, Metropolitan Museum of Art

hamar jigarwa se bhi, uu saans lutal
hamar suratiya okar aina mein terdha

My mother walks to the Ganesh statue, drawn
to its bronze, an image once stolen, now in the public

domain. Once he perched in Tamil Nadu. Once he sat
on Mount Meru. Once he was tin and copper. Once

my mother's mother knew her real name before
planters heated her and poured her into sand.

Return me to the desh, cross the sea, to our river?
Where do Pargana village's wheat fields green? Who knows—

Colonization still erases our memories.
Ma sings shards of prayer—*siri guru charan*—

to gods broken from temples, dancing gods cut down
at the feet, mounted uptown on 86th street.

They even steal the breath from our throats;
in their mirror our faces warp.

Guyana

Guinea?

          New Guinea?

  Ghana?

      Gatineau?

Gaza?

            Gaya—like Bodhgaya?

    Guadalupe?

        Guatemala?

Guyamas?

              Guelph?

      Guiana?

अ ā इ ई उ ऊ

ए ऐ ओ औ ऋ

क ख ग gha ङ

cha छ ज झ ञ

ta ठ da ढ -

त थ da dha न

प फ ब भ म

य र ल व

श ष sa ह

So de fool dem people an' bring 'am come. How de catch 'am? De been tell dem dat abi go nuddah country an' a-you go get plenty job, a-you go get 'nuff money from cut cane, a-you go live happy. An' India mein dem been a-punish. Wuk tiday you get food tiday, an' you know tomorrow dem starve. So dem been a-haunted ti come away. An' when dem bring 'am dem na get house, dem na get nutin', dem a-cut cane. Dem a-punish bad. But wha' you go do? When me family been come dis country dem been very poor. All India-man been poor. None na been rich.

Inaugural Poem with Silence

We know exactly how this happened:
two out of every three white folks want me dead.

Orange clouds worry. Another night
I tithe my lilac hope. Today

hounds release hell along roads,
those hiding in the underbrush scatter.

White boys beat a Saudi student to death.

Klansmen march North Carolina streets,
a mouth with white hats like teeth—

On the walls of my high school:
better start picking y'all slave numbers KKK.

In Oviedo, twenty miles
from Sanford, even in Honolulu

a student scribbles.

In my beautiful country, some will die mid-prayer.

Terrorism in Manhattan

pani mein chini milijai asaani
garam masalawa mein mirchiya kali

The white officers question the hijabi
woman with a bag of basmati in burlap,

What's in the bag? They understand the *basmati*—
Thank the Merciful God—the world is palm sized.

They rub her with paper strips to see if
the grains she cradles as a son will shoot into

green stalks or bombs. Her cousin disappeared several
years ago; no one remembers the lilt of his du'a.

She wonders where the line is to ask her own fire-
queries. Who did they wipe when home grown terrorists

shot up her mosque?

In water sugar mixes easily,
in garam masala, black pepper.

Massacre Ballad

in memoriam of August 5th, 2012 and of Paramjit Kaur, Satwant Singh Kaleka,
Prakash Singh, Sita Singh, Ranjit Singh, and Suveg Singh

suraj bhail chanda, bhor bhail kara
amrika mein aayieke ham bhaili sikara

I didn't hide, but wove cowries into
my beard. My brother retreated to his Bible;

smeared his skin in paint and cried, *We're not like them.*
My sister wept for the return of the Queen,

swearing Her Majesty still watches after
her overseas darkies. My father was growing

linen and cotton fibers to weave a spangled
banner as his shroud. My mother clove her tongue,

misspoke her name and shut her guru's door tight
against her own child. She returned to starching

stained undershirts that absorb the toil
of who the newscasters called *real* Americans.

The sun is moon-colored, the dawn pitch,
coming to America we have become prey.

Indo-Queer II

DOMA *gir gail, mubarak, sab* backra fag *ke*
phir bhi crabdog *marela dagariyan pe*

What kind of antiman staggers from the straight
man's blow, the aunty asks, *the bad kind in cutoffs, who*

dance wildness as children watch—or the good
ones who regret their sins? What of the kind, curbside

gushing from the head? See those pavement stains, blots
of cinnabar and wine, read the abir as Vedas or

tea leaves: sanguine crimes morphing as they ride mouth
to mouth, until stories catch fire and *fall inside*

de cane. He went down on the street before the bar
with rainbow flags for eyes. Boys—before you come out

in heels, open your blinds. Thirsty spirits of hate-
spiced rum traipse Liberty Ave and Jamaica.

> *DOMA fell, congrats to all the white fags,*
> *but still crabdogs are beaten on the streets*

Fire Rass

paas aaye okar hathan se kuchu bhi nahi lebe
leye ta ram jane toke ka bimari pardijai

To keep jumbie an' so out, folks throw long rice grains
beyond doorsteps. Behind palms hear them gyaff,

'E go suck a nex' one blood come night. Before blazing
the dancehall, we sneak out our windows to stash skins

in coconut shells, hung from maple branches—
It's easy to sheath the body in flares, in latex

in the disco. Keys twisted in holes as a fetish,
parents fear sons will drink nights stiff under neon

marquee lights, or that we'll peel off our shirts in public
toilets, or hack up flames. They root out our grounds,

rub peppers in our skin's sores. Once we're outed,
they'll set us on fire, write songs on our pyres.

> *If you get close, take nothing from their hands—*
> *God knows what diseases you will contract.*

Shame in Mathura

ratiya mein radha ke paas jaila kanha
baki rukhmini ke gaale dale jaimala

Madho, you shake like the earth, thrashing and
foaming at the lips the night you sip malathion

to expel field insects from your guts. The elders
and priest tie your dupatta to your bride's

sari. You writhe on the bedclothes that
sponged the sweat of last night's men, setting free

your *oh gods* to the air like wraiths. The doctors
mine your chest; excavate your rachis and vane, cast

the queer catch into the sea but it grows a macaw plume.
The fourth time you drink poison, your father

binds you to the bedpost, gagged; drags you lashed,
to the mandap and from each pore rips your feathers.

At night Krishna goes to Radha,
but he placed the wedding garland on Rukmini's neck.

Siren

rum okar premika hoye, oke ka parwah hojai
aakaas se pathar gire, prithvi mar-pit sahani

The secret to return from the brink is not to
swim slowly up the waterways, skin the color

of brackish canals; to disavow the heavy hands
of men. She sings murder ballads as lullabies

to her twins in the planting season. Every
sea cow alive bears scars carved by speeding men.

Her first calf a willow tree; the second, swings an axe,
determined to gash his wife's back with steel.

Mother tells the legend of Nani's looking glass:
a good wife, the moon, was once a chunk of earth.

First, the discord of vocal folds, seven lives
bad luck, then forever to spit ballads from her eyes.

If rum is his lover, what does he care?
If stones fall from the sky, the earth takes the beating.

Outcry

In memoriam of Rajwantie Baldeo

A twist of cotton
daubed in oil
catches flame, an echo

of starlight whose fire
you will enter
as if the trial

were not your husband's,
named *Prem* which means
love, with his machete

hands who cut you down
after claiming to pay
your passage to Liberty

Avenue, from whose breath,
amber with rum,
a demon springs

into limb and shadow
and spits knives;
he bruised you plenty

before but the neighbors
closed their blinds,
silenced mantras that led

from falsehood
to truth, from dusk
to light and turned up

their Soca Chutney,
now you lay, Bahini,
a red river mouth,

Sita swallowed by the earth
proving her chastity
to Ram who betrays her.

Last night at Naresa's
see the Queens-
neighbors gather, each one

clutching a candle
but it's too late to chant
sarve bhadrani pashyantu

may all be free of suffering
or for me to say
I've lit my clay lamp

and you are the flicker
I shield with this poem.

अ ā इ ई उ ऊ

ए ऐ ओ औ ऋ

क ख ग gha ङ

cha छ ज झ ञ

ट ठ ड ढ ण

त थ द dha न

प फ ब भ ma

य र ल व

श ष sa ह

Their hands blistered contract ink, fingerprints the poet's mark on hilts of hammered steel. They talk story with a sharp hack. They sing as they cleave stalks and air. They mangle eye and hand alike. The word *mangle* sounds like *mangal*, Hindi for auspicious. The word *machete* is the son of *macho*. In Pap's garage his own rusts until it bleeds.

Neemakharam

My trusting love, my father,
feet still warm from circling
the sacred fire, poured

burnt engine oil
into a gopher tortoise's hole,
the earth drank its blood.

He planted an orange tree
meters away. Its fruit was night,
so he drowned it in blue

crystals meant to fertilize
but its leaves browned. Instead
of blessing it, he cursed

the son his body made—
May you never bear fruit;
May you be thrown out, trampled by men—

I am all salt and salt-less.
What can oil-soaked earth bear? God
the father sang me a lullaby,

Neemakharam, neemakharam
I've given you the kingdom;
you've given me a snake.

My simple love, give me
the swallow of your chest and I will
crush it in my fist.

Indo-Queer III

kalapani paar kare bides jaye khatir
urdat pakshiya prem ke rang mein khojaye

With your first Guyanese you relax your tongue,
don't lock your closet doors when you light the stove

trying to keep the curry out of your cotton.
He wonders, *Is this what it's like for everyone else?*

as he breaks one hundred glass churdiya against
the grey wall of your Little India walk-up.

The rainbow shards in your sole erupt from the skin's
surface as birds of paradise, hungry beaks open.

You feed them threads of folksongs from your silk
bruises and you open the windows. Falling in the cane field

you rouge your face. It's too late. The bottle drank
him whole and his jamun berries stain your skin.

Crossing the Black Seas for a foreign country
the flying bird loses its bearings in love's colors.

Sudama

for Hari Alluri

hamar naam ke yaad karo bhagwan
hiya aaike ham toke pukarat hai

With beaten rice or sattu—all his possessions
bound in cloth, he limps shoeless, bleeding

to Dwarka, wrapped in devotion, birds purloining
frayed threads from his shirt for their weavings.

O Krishna, O puppeteer of sorrow
and joy, in this conflict of yours and mine

what space between the maya of gold and brass
comes friendship? Look. I have torn my soles wandering.

Hearing, The Blue Lord washes Sudama's feet
in tears and eats the scant gift of crushed paddies—

Yet I wonder if Sudama were not born a brahmin,
what god would transform his hut into palace?

My name, remember, Lord
I am here calling out to you.

Lyre

kanha ke dhun phelat hai charo oriya
aasun ke dariya bahewat hai balamwa

There is no trace of you in the cold bedclothes,
no hair, no stains. You are not on my hands for days.

I caught a slight bunting with lawa, puffed rice,
and the seed of another I spit out on my knees—

When in my palm it lit, I trapped it in the porch
bucket where slithered a caged water moccasin.

I tell you the truth that I am a liar, my heart
a wreath braided of sheep gut. When you find out

the name of the man I took, you slash cords,
you hurl the frame into the river—sever strings of steel

and sinew. Vega, Sulafat, Kepler, all misaligned;
I extend my wings when the dawn's curtain rises.

Krishna's tune spreads in four directions
my lover causes this river of tears to flow.

OK, Cupid

he ram, he isa, kam dev ke ka jaduwa hai
ke computer *ke* onlineiya *jaye saiya se mil jai*

Too much whiskey, I go to meet the man whose
thumbnail I've clicked and clicked. But I make it late

to the date. On the train I feel the pretty
Queens-queers eyeing me, blood about to boil

over buttoned jeans and then in my pharynx.
I down brown men who bic their pubes, who whirl like

ribbons on sticks. Souse-stumbling I stare back at
Trini dreads who grab their dicks—

track them behind subway maps on the platform.
Flip a gold coin and see. Heads to meet alone. Tails,

Little India. Some top in temple and church,
my predate fuck tops and I take it best I can.

O Ram, O Jesus, what is the magic of Kama Deva
that online you will meet your beloved?

Indo-Queer IV

for Sundari

dudh rahe dudh aur pani rahe pani
urdat pakshi ke rang kaun dekh sakela

Hear your Aji talk, *Beta, you na get sense?*
Hear your Nani say, *Chach, you head na gi' you wuk?*

When the elders gather they will all clap their hands,
they will beg your rainbowed silks to wave

and wave. I've seen it in Queens, at the Rajkumari
Center in curls, in kajal, in a lehenga.

You dance-walk to buskers' beats down Liberty
the A train and E, to rum an' Coke and your wine,

with five countries in your migration story.
You still na get shame, your father rum-stunned snores,

though your mother cries for two years straight after
she finds another man's underwear in your laundry.

Milk remains milk, water, water,
who can make out the flying bird's colors?

अ ā i ī - ऊ

e ऐ ओ औ ri

क kh ग gha ङ

च छ ज झ ञ

ta tha da - na

- थ - - न

प pha ब भ म

ya र ल व

- - sa ha

Coolie Oddity

Jahaji opened palms and veins:
>   cane leaf, palm tree. Arkot talk:
we Jesus water; your sweat
>   into gold. And in the part: blood,

an ocean gasp, spit salt:
>   haze cape and southern populations
foam and shadow under surf
>   ace, Paati's ghost, hemorrhaging

birth: trauma, absolute, shoulders
>   broad back, boarded back and
Bach in barracks and psalms blistered
>   with soot and mud in Skeldon

de crappeau spit 'pon de punt trench
>   an' koker close and open,
its malaria-mouthed yawn. Her arms
>   covered in tattooed names of men.

See the grass warp into cane
>   straws sucking water and sweat,
he cries out for you, Sriji;
>   drops a smile:

confused by Hindu sense of time, the kalpas and Kalis who destroy all but Kalki who rides the horse, so who would celebrate May 5th as *Indian Arrival Day*, that day when our contracts with destitution began and I've stopped expecting teleological refrains or a time stamp or any indication of what cycle I am on other than a folksong, which keeps time and tells us what is new or different based on the fading of Hindi or the greatening of English either through word substitution or by inclusion of a paratactic chorus, or like how the word *antiman* stands in for *hijra* but means *gandu* or

Ritual: spill milk in the water

                    a white ghost against brown

pills of sea men flake off chest hair

                    fuck off just here. An' de man a vex:

gwan da side. gwan da side.

                    Abi dis gan a farren

typed right here: lings::lunds::lolos

                    under saris, under ordhnies.

magistrates check for dicks;

                    lift sheets of men at night::

[the stink of charred foreskin]::

                    sodomites, so they might dole

punyshment with brands and it's why

                    we left our fosse, this is where

they cleft our ulnas. Why mummah

                    an' puppah hol' de Bible tight tight.

In cane fields fed
by hacked corpses

queers lost queers
to missions evil and gist

read oddity for odyssey
a lesson an identifier

to Christian-identitize

anti/rass/batty//bwoy/man

gand//u/walla

Eh antiman. De Lord Jesus tell me you does tek man on Sunday and nevah go church. You nasee fe days. Come out de house, de police cyan't save you.

In the pansy's pants, they tie
an ordhni and night smile an' gawe:

ruko ruko sriji
    sankar ke pyari mohini
adam roj charawe aarti
    shiv–sankar ke ling ki
phele karo ling puja
    phir karo kaam dubara.

lived in Jaipur, I went back to India over a century after Sriji left from Khidderpore (or wherever the East India Company set up shop); sitting in Anokhi Café I ordered coffee and a bourgeois chocolate muffin, baked in a western oven; yet the greatest surprise I encountered was the packet of sugar stuffed into the canister of condiments and additives that read *Unrefined Demerara* and I could see myself, how I have lived in India all this time—Guyanese, some source of labor, unnecessary, unrefined, forgotten like

How I love a man-

                    stalk. Cain ousted and
death most certain.

                    See this mark?

                              *

a bow strung of sari silk,
strands of your hair

                    violence bowed into blossoms

a bow strung of sari silk,
strands of queerhair

                    violin bowed into blossom::

the skin: a beak parts,
a river lolls like flame-tongue::

                    a sugar field scored
with Coolie notes
cleffed with salt.

bahut pahile ke batiya hai. langtime mein laikan sari bandke naache rahe. kabhi bibah ke time uu dulha ke mai-baap ke aage naache rahe aur koi nahi mana karal. aur guyana mein aaike hamlog oise kare chordeli kaheki langtime ke rail chali gail. he ram, ham ka kare? eh babuwa, courantyne ke paar kareke ta tu jaroor launda ke naach dekhbe, suriname mein ii tarah ke purani baat jari hai. aur ham sun rakhili ki nu yack mein ek-go jawaan jahaji-putr launda ke naach maut ke munh se bachayal aur ab uu hiya sari, lehenga, choli, ordhni pehnke langtime ke jhanda utharela.

Stop, Stop Sriji, Shiva fucks
Mohini. Men raise offerings daily
to his mighty prick. First worship
then worship the cock again.

My body's a packet of Demerara
on a Jaipur table. Rip me split.
Queer me open with your teeth,
a cane stalk spits from my lips.

```
a    ā    i    ī    -    ū

     e    -    o    -    -

ka   kh   ga   gha   -

   cha   -   ja   -   -

ta   tha   da   dha   -

      -    -    -    -    na

pa   pha   ba   -   ma

   ya   ra   la   wa

      -    -    sa   ha
```

People a-knock drum an' sing de own kine song. Dem been know fe play good music an' enjoy it too. Langtime you dance by de drum wha' you a-play: de dholak an' de dantaal an' de majira. Da get one separate kine sound. Jus' you hear da sound an' you know how fe dance you git up right away an' you start. Na mattah who an' who a-watch. Dance, dance, naacho.

Dantaal, an Instrument

adi tala: dhā ki ta tā ki ta dhā ti ta
ka ti ta tā ti ra ki ta ga di ga na

Sakhiya, if we forget our songs and stories
who will we become? Consider the dholak player.

Consider his chutney. The drummer knocks
this rhythm deep into us: talas in our temples,

a heartbeat to keep the deep time of the ocean's
lapping, to keep us clapping, to keep us

remembering our names. Gold music of the hand's
bangles. I made a pair of my own: pointed rods

marked in Xs and flowers, to gleam in tempo,
the top smooth and bare before curved to fit the wrist.

Friends, beat a drum yourselves, become time-keepers:
iron oxcart axles transformed into music.

Chutney Mashup

aaj sawaliya ham na jaibe bhitar
balma, ulat pavan chal gaya, chadar bichao

You tie your veil to meet me in the courtyard,
though there no neem tree grows. You wrap your limbs

tightly about mine as jamun fruits betray
their pedicels and stain the concrete with ruby wine.

The shehnai weeps for us only; inside
my strength has ebbed. Spread a sheet on the earth, balma,

that when weary we may lie on silk in peace.
Despite your wise restraint your morals will scatter

in a fire dance—what god can save us?
I will never escape the body's betrayal.

The neighbor women jeer at the stains on my veil,
my ruined fabric I pleat and tuck at my waist.

Today, love, I will not go outside.
Love, against the backwards wind, spread a sheet.

81

Bollywood Confabulation

Look at your feet, so beautiful. Do
not step on the ground, filth will smear them;

your future will fill with pricks. He with
a fearful heart, understand dead. Death will dance

on your head—lift your eyes and see. I am
its servant, thirsty from birth; you my jewels

my raiment. I redden my part, adorn
myself for my beloved, terrified

of evil-eye so with kohl I streak
my waterline. Petals shrivel but thorns

stay sharp. Your lips' tremor is morning; when
you let loose your tresses, midnight. What place

has fear if barbs do not dread withering?
Love brings ruin and ruins lives—

Guide

In the desert if I say *Ram*
or *Rahim* will the clouds break
into a steady drum? If sky cracks

I will sing for you, stamp
my feet into ribbon. What if I said
even in the night

where your hair's perfume
torments, *I am still parched?*
There are no lowly births,

clouds too begin first as sea.
Would you believe
that I could leave the world,

drawn up by the sun
as a saint, me, a sham of a man?
I watched you dance

like a cobra—what does it take
to be so bewitched by spirit?

I spend the dark
with whiskey, making a mask
of withered roses. How quickly

a shadow can pass
and you become a stranger.

Folksong

ek-go tikaana ke khoj mein urdeli
jangal jangal gujarke, hamar muluk nahin

You drown in a flood of birdsong; don't trouble
with lyrics. The body is disjoint; warbler

and robin, children of broken eggs. How long
can the belly hold a flame, lighting perch to perch

in sage migration? Take these petals of joy.
Place them on your tongue. Something inside does not

still. A cardinal flame lights into dicot
fireworks. This is your chest. This is your garden.

Searching for a single perch I wing
jungle to jungle; I have no country.

Kabira

for Amar Ramessar

hathailiyan ke mehndi halki hoike gayaab—
ii sarirwa mein bhala kaa tikaav

You will your house of clay and breath
a fortress. One day, ash and smoke will play fire

games in the courtyard. Remember this hovel
is of five senses—

Does wind stay trapped in a room when its windows
yawn? Without country it flows as river-water,

a traceless origin. How can this structure
of earth and bone be home? Says Kabir, *However*

beautiful—gold or silver—when the cage
door cracks what bird stays inside?

The palm's mehndi lightens then disappears—
what permanence is in your body?

Directions to the Holy Place

for Rushi Vyas

agar ii mritlok sab maya hoye ta
tohar andar se kekar anjora chamkela

You watch beetles worm from the mouths of saints,
words rotting in books. Breath swims your capillaries

and exits your lips. You emerge to the asphalt
avenue; bow your shoes against the concrete web

of veins in night's hush. You hold a light to
a street sign; peel your eyes for an augury.

Tied to your throat, an amulet—its symbols
in a script you are illiterate to, a hare

ensnared by runaway thirst. Since, you've opened
your seven doors don't lace holy words about

your waist, afraid on the twelfth-hour path. You are
a pulse of star through samsara, a firefly beat.

If this is a world of illusion then
whose light shines from within you?

Indo-Queer V

barsaat mein dariya samundar bane
behet nadiya bhala kaun rok paiye

Against the trade winds your Aji teaches you
the force of her songs; you sing in her voice but your

family still disowns you. Your puas roost
around a table and black-tongue you with curses

like marbles thrown to trip you, to split your head
on the cement. They are vexed you survive; that you

rise up from the pavement to voice strains on how
to be expelled, to cross the kalapani of

uncertainty, how to thrive in diaspora,
the sun flaring in your chest. In this time of fading

convective movement transforms you into
deity: The Mincing God, The God Giver of Flame.

> *In the monsoon the river floods into a sea,*
> *who can possibly arrest a river's flow?*

May 5, 1838

perwa ke daar par hamar potiya jhulai
abse log hamke bulawe jai jahaj-bhai

On those first ships did they know their ash
applied evenly fertilizes the land-grant fields?

We are wreckage, broken planks, history's skipping
record—repeating the migrant strain again

and against kalapani ke twist-up face while
the rakshas of erasure licks its lips. *What's born of death—*

guyana se nikale hiya aaye khatir
langtime now me lef' da' side fe come yah-so.

Here we grow wild. In Queens, see clumps of bora,
long beans wind feral by fire hydrants.

We sow bits of ourselves in all corners:
flags on bamboo posts, milk poured into the sea.

> *My grand-daughter will swing on the tree branch,*
> *we will all call you Brother of the Ship.*

अ – – – –

– – – –

क – – –

– – – –

– थ – –

– – – –

– – – –

य – –

– – –

We Come in Planes

after Mahadai Das

samundar ke par karke aaili
    hamlog hawai jahaj par baitke
anguti chhap lagaike grimitiya
    bhaili dubara. dagariya
se naua khet mein hamlog

kantrak se bandhal. tufan
    hamar ghar nast
karai ke baad, amriki samaj
    hamar gardan pe khardal hai.
uu pani je hamlog ke chatela

ujar rang hamlog pe
    lagawe hai. kheti git, calypso,
aur Chutney-Soca oisan gawe,
    matti, hamlog chale jai berbice,
essequibo, aur demerara se

jfk aur mia tak chale jai. sona
    koi ke bulawe hai. kai log
jumbie, churail, cutlish ke kate se
    daraike hiya aaile. koi garib
haal mein majburi se aaile.

We come in planes
    sliding down the long tongues
of runways. Across the seas
    we come indentured again by
fingerprints, to a new plantation,

to the Republic, that stands
    on our throats after hurricanes
dust our homes to toothpicks.
    What laps hulls, laps us
too in white. Cane-cutting

songs, calypso and Chutney-
    Soca sing out, *Matti, my people,*
come leh we go from Berbice,
    Essequibo, Demerara to
JFK and MIA. Some come

snake-charmed by gold, some
    frightened of jumbie, churail,
and cutlass chop, some
    come away unable to wait
for money to reach

mai-bap ek-go chhatra ke visa
    uu dono ke bich mein aaile,
lutheran log ke daya se bandhe.
    aapan munh bakra ke ujar bhail
pardhe khatir hiya aaike.

choral dharti par ham aapan aji
    ke dhusar akhiyan se
vada karali ke ham aapan gaathaagit
    baje rahab dholak bajaike.
1838 ke bhut je hesperus

aur whitby ke sawar rahe
    hamke paresan karela kaheki
uu bhut, daru aur mar-pit ke awtar leila.
    hamar purakh log okar mukut
ke hira rahe, choral koh-i-nur jaisan.

gladstone hamar nam
    Bound Coolie likhal, chini ke bimari
se bandhak rahe taki
    hamke aapan naam ke yaad
na aa saki hai, okar sewa mein.

from foreign. Ma and Pap
    one student visa between them,
whitened their tongues, crossed
    kalapani, bound to the mercy
of dunkay damn Lutherans.

On stolen land I promised
    Aji's grey eyes to beat
dholak to her ballads
    that sprout feathers.
Ghosts of 1838 aboard

the *Hesperus and Whitby*, haunt
    as spirits and cuttings;
our ancestors, the projects
    of the crown gemmed with
the *stolen mountain of light*.

Gladstone rewrote
    our names as *Bound Coolie*—
bound for sugared amnesia.
    Who will recall Par-Aji's
silver anklets, the logies

94

Who go remembah Par-Aji ke
    kardha an' de logie wha' stay
til dat side, pass Coribahtan?
    Who go know fe sing
Aji ke rice planting song

an' when she lef' she maike
    an' na look whe' she been
step? Or who go call Nani name
    when she talk *bush been deh
all about?* An' de woman

who man cut out she
    nose fe mek a jaimala?
In Queens, Coolie woman
    does still punish an' a Libahty,
dem lungera does sell a cutlish

gi' you fe buy. Man still does
    chap 'e wife an' gyalfrien' fe so,
middle a de road, na mattah sun
    a shine an' who an' who a pass.
Hear langtime people been talk

now farther away than
    Corriverton? Who knows
the tune of Aji's rice field
    planting song of how she left
her mother's home and never

turned to salt? Or what
    Nani saw when *bush been
deh all about?* Or the garlands
    men string about their necks
of women's severed noses?

In Queens, still, Coolie
    women's blood cries out
from the field and from Liberty
    where big cutlish sell
in the shops, where lungera

men hack at their wives
    despite daylight. Hear the old
time people say, *Wha' deh in rum—
    nutin' na deh. Me go tek one
drink now an' go drunk,*

daru mein kuch,
*   kuch na hai. tab daru pili*
ab drunk hain,
*   le ke cutlish ab doraila,*
beta ke beti ke,

sab ke mare dorila,
*   ta kaun phaida, beta?*
One hundred year a pass
    an' abi paper done.
Abi come dis side boung.

Hiya, de goung na de bakra
    ke groung. 'E been tief'am
an' compel abi dis fe stan cana he.
    Abi one new kine jahaj: hawai
jahaji bhai bahin, Matti, abi dis

been a crass de sea an' de lan',
    de rivah, an' de jungle. Abi dis
a been deh pan de fiyah:
    come leh abi tie bundle,
one matti na abi dis?

me go tek a cutlish an' run.
*   Me go run fe chop an' kill*
me pickni dem.
*   Me run fe kill all bady,*
so wha' good deh in 'am?

A century has passed since
    our first contracts crumbled,
logies and whip abolished.
    Our bent minds made a holiday
of our arrival into bondage.

In the North, we blossoms
    of jahajis, settle Native land
however driven—
    birthed of air: Hawai Jahaj
Bhai-Bahin, siblings

of the plane. Matti, crossers
    of desert, of sea, of sky,
of jungle, crossers of flame:
    let's tie bundles together,
link strings and fingers.

We never allied against
　　British planters who trapped us.
What bones remain unbroken
　　from soil thick with boulders—
How they possessed us

with spirits of rum and anti-
　　Blackness. Erect statues cast
our stilled horror, of jahajis
　　and masters. In their shadows,
still we come, now together.

We come, milk-fattened
　　on lies, surveilled and profiled,
told to hate who America hates
　　to spy on our neighbor or exile,
this fire-trial or the deportation,

the reach ICE, an actioning arm
　　of white supremacy. What you do
at dusk crows like Peter's cock,
　　no cover will fool us. America,
hear, every rope has two ends

one pliant the other serpent, watch
    us pen eyeliner, tie the Hudson
as a sari, flick the pallu over
    our shoulders to damn empire.
I will never bow before whitelash,

my knees will never kiss cement;
    me go stan' jus so me deh. Hear
good, our skin teeth na laugh.
    Dear America, the moon runs
until the sun catches it.

Notes

"Cutlish" (as a long poem between sections) adapts words from my Aji: née Bhagwati Singh / Gangadai Mohabir.

"The Po-Co Kid" uses lines from Gayatri Chakravorty Spivak's "Can the Subaltern Speak" translated into Guyanese Bhojpuri.

"Dove (Tell Me the Number of Your Plane)" takes its title and half of the first line from the Sundar Popo song "A Scorpion Sting Meh."

"Sapera, the Snake Charmer" uses words from Psalm 58:3-5.

"Falling from a Plane" takes its title from the Sundar Popo song "Don't Fall in Love."

"Curry Powder" uses the chorus from the song "Curry Powder Se Banaye Tarkari" by Mangroo Badal.

"Hiranyagarbha" uses words from Sylvia Plath's "Thalidomide."

"Snowfall in the Tropics" uses lines from Wordsworth's poem "I Wandered Lonely as a Cloud."

"Offering" uses words from Surendra Gambhir's doctoral dissertation *The East Indian Speech Community in Guyana: A Sociolinguistic Study with Special Reference to Koine Formation"* which was conducted in my father's birth-village of Crabwood Creek, Berbice, Guyana.

"South Asian Art Exhibit" uses lyrics from the Hanuman Chalisa prayer purported to be written by Tulsidas.

"Indo-Queer II" quotes from Sundar Popo's song "Kaise Bani."

In "Fire Rass" twisting keys in doors, throwing rice outside protects humans against this type of blood-sucking fire monster. Fire Rass hide their human skins at night and wander about looking to prey upon the unsuspecting.

"Outcry" responds to the quote by Nadia Bourne, a NYC-based activist who says, "Rajwantie Baldeo was viciously murdered...And where was the outcry from our community? Did we hear anything at our kitchen tables? Did we hear anything at our mandirs [temples]?" in the article "New York's Indo-Caribbean Community Honors its Victims of Domestic Violence" in *Repeating Islands*.

"Coolie Oddity" speaks of the indentureship of hijras from India to the Caribbean and the bonded labor of who we would call today queer folks.

"Chutney Mashup" is comprised of parts of chutney songs in Caribbean Hindi. The English in the poem are fragments of my own translations of those songs.

"Bollywood Confabulation" uses words and phrases from my own translations of songs from the films "Pakeezah," "Sholay," "Mughal-e-Azam," "Sahib, Bibi, aur Ghulam," and "Kabhi Kabhi."

"Guide" is based on the 1965 film starring Dev Anand and Waheeda Rehman.

"May 5th 1838" was the date that the first ships carrying indentured laborers arrived in Guyana carrying 396 Indians aboard from Bengal and Bihar.

"We Came In Planes" is after Mahadai Das's poem "They Came In Ships" and uses phrases from *The East Indian Speech Community in Guyana: A Sociolinguistic Study with Special Reference to Koine Formation* by Surendra Gambhir.

Aja/Aji: paternal grandfather/grandmother

chutney: a relish made of mango and spices; a style of Indo-Caribbean music

daal: lentils

dantaal: from *danda* "stick" and *tala* "rhythm"; a percussive instrument made from the axle of an oxcart used to keep time in Indo-Caribbean music

dupatta: a scarf

jaggery: reduced sugarcane

jahaji: "people of the ship," those Coolies that traveled to the British colonies by ship from India

kajal: kohl

kalapani: "black water," the ocean that once crossed erases caste and ties to India

launda ke naach: an old style of dance where men perform as women; (boy's dance)

lehenga: a skirt and blouse outfit

limin': hanging out

malathion: a type of pesticide

mandap: the stage where the pandit performs the Hindu wedding ceremony

ordhni: a woman's veil tucked into the waistband and wrapped around the shoulders and to the back of the head

rakshas: a type of Hindu demon

Ram Ram: a Hindu greeting in Indo-Caribbean space, the reduplication of the name of a god

wine: to wind, a type of pelvic Caribbean dance

Acknowledgments

Versions of these poems appeared in these journals:

Anti-, The Asian American Literary Review, Asymptote Journal, Crab Orchard Review, DIAGRAM, The Feminist Wire, Figure 1, Foglifter, Hawai'i Review, Kenyon Review, Los Angeles Review, The Margins, Mistake House Magazine, Newtown Literary Journal, The Pacific Review, POETRY Magazine, Posit Journal, Prairie Schooner, The Rumpus, Small Axe: A Platform for Caribbean Criticism, South Dakota Review, Spiral Orb, Split This Rock, Storyscape Journal, Tupelo Quarterly Review, and *wildness.*

"Tell Me the Number of Your Plane" appears in *Best American Poetry 2015* as "Dove"
"Kalapani" first appears in the anthology *Go Home! Twenty-Four Journeys from the Asian American Writers' Workshop and Feminist Press*
"Bollywood Confabulation" first appears in the anthology *Reel Verse*

Special thanks to Martha Rhodes, Ryan Murphy, Clarissa Long, Bridget Bell, Hannah Matheson, and the folks at Four Way Books for their continued support, editorial guidance, and belief in my work.

Gratitude to Anya Backlund, Alison Granucci, Miyako Hannan-Scarponi, Barbara Fenig, Ana Paula Simōnes, Linda Banks Molina, and Shannon Hearn at Blue Flower Arts.

A world of gratitude to Nicole Cooley who told me to write what frightened me, for her found poems, and for her kind words about this book; to Kimiko Hahn for her keen eyes and loving mentoring; and to Roger Sedarat for his experimentations with translation and form. Thank you to Allison Adelle Hedge Coke who believes in a world that I want to live in, filled with love and respect for all beings. Thanks also to Patrick Rosal and Jericho Brown for their kindness and words.

Thank you to the invaluable communities of the Caribbean Equality Project, the Indo-Caribbean Alliance, Kundiman, and to the faculty and staff at Emerson College.

Thank you to: Saiya Baba (Silas), the Joneses, Mohabirs, Anjani Prashad, Jodi Miles, Sarah, Justin, Will, and Rosie McIver, Tanzila Ahmed, Charmila Ajmera, Kazim Ali, Hari Alluri, Mohamed Q. Amin, Ryan Artes, Andre Bagoo, Neelanajana Banerjee, Kay Ulanday Barrett, Chaya Bhuvaneswar, Justin Bigos, Amalia Bueno, Lawrence-Minh Bùi Davis, Robindra Deb, William Depoo, Patrick Donnelly, Tina Edan, Richard Georges, Will Nu'utupu Giles, Sundari Indian Goddess, Rigoberto González, Andil Gosine, Jaimie Gusman, Joseph Han, Ian Harnarine, Corinne and Jon Hyde, Elizabeth Jaikaran, Tara Jayakar, Janine Joseph, Lee Kava, Mimi Khúc, Devi Laskar, Dan Lau, Nicholas Laughlin, Kenji Liu, Neha Longani, Janet McAdams, Shikha Saklani Malaviya, Nadia Misir, Faisal Mohyuddin, Cheryl Naruse, Craig Santos Perez, Divya M. Persaud, Shivanee Ramlochan, Amar Ramessar, No'u Revilla, Barbara Jane Reyes, Lee Ann Roripaugh, Kenrick Ross, Anjoli Roy, Sreshtha Sen, Harold Schechter, Rashmi Sharma, Erin Stalcup, Adeeba Shahid Talukder, Rushi Vyas, Katie Williams, and Suzanne Wulach.

Finally, to Enkidu Shehrni, to Kajal Sahmi, and to Jordan Andrew Miles, thank you.

Rajiv Mohabir, an immigrant to the United States, is the author of
The Cowherd's Son (Tupelo Press 2017, winner of the 2015 Kundiman
Prize; Eric Hoffer Honorable Mention 2018) and *The Taxidermist's Cut*
(Four Way Books 2016, winner of the Four Way Books Intro to Poetry
Prize, Finalist for the Lambda Literary Award for Gay Poetry in 2017),
and translator of *I Even Regret Night: Holi Songs of Demerara* (1916)
(Kaya Press 2019) which received a PEN/Heim Translation Fund Grant
Award and the 2020 Harold Morton Landon Translation Award from
the American Academy of Poets. His memoir *Antiman* (Restless Books
2021) received the New Immigrant Writing Prize in 2019. He received
his PhD in English from the University of Hawai'i, Mānoa and his MFA
in poetry from Queens College, CUNY. Currently he is an Assistant
Professor of poetry in the MFA program at Emerson College. He lives in
the Boston area.

Publication of this book was made possible by grants and donations. We are also grateful to those individuals who participated in our 2020 Build a Book Program. They are:

Anonymous (14), Robert Abrams, Nancy Allen, Maggie Anderson, Sally Ball, Matt Bell, Laurel Blossom, Adam Bohannon, Lee Briccetti, Therese Broderick, Jane Martha Brox, Christopher Bursk, Liam Callanan, Anthony Cappo, Carla & Steven Carlson, Paul & Brandy Carlson, Renee Carlson, Cyrus Cassells, Robin Rosen Chang, Jaye Chen, Edward W. Clark, Andrea Cohen, Ellen Cosgrove, Peter Coyote, Janet S. Crossen, Kim & David Daniels, Brian Komei Dempster, Matthew DeNichilo, Carl Dennis, Patrick Donnelly, Charles Douthat, Morgan Driscoll, Lynn Emanuel, Monica Ferrell, Elliot Figman, Laura Fjeld, Michael Foran, Jennifer Franklin, Sarah Freligh, Helen Fremont & Donna Thagard, Reginald Gibbons, Jean & Jay Glassman, Ginny Gordon, Lauri Grossman, Naomi Guttman & Jonathan Mead, Mark Halliday, Beth Harrison, Jeffrey Harrison, Page Hill Starzinger, Deming Holleran, Joan Houlihan, Thomas & Autumn Howard, Elizabeth Jackson, Christopher Johanson, Voki Kalfayan, Maeve Kinkead, David Lee, Jen Levitt, Howard Levy, Owen Lewis, Jennifer Litt, Sara London & Dean Albarelli, David Long, James Longenbach, Excelsior Love, Ralph & Mary Ann Lowen, Jacquelyn Malone, Donna Masini, Catherine McArthur, Nathan McClain, Richard McCormick, Victoria McCoy, Ellen McCulloch-Lovell, Judith McGrath, Debbie & Steve Modzelewski, Rajiv Mohabir, James T. F. Moore, Beth Morris, John Murillo & Nicole Sealey, Michael & Nancy Murphy, Maria Nazos, Kimberly Nunes, Bill O'Brien, Susan Okie & Walter Weiss, Rebecca Okrent, Sam Perkins, Megan Pinto, Kyle Potvin, Glen Pourciau, Kevin Prufer, Barbara Ras, Victoria Redel, Martha Rhodes, Paula Rhodes, Paula Ristuccia, George & Nancy Rosenfeld, M. L. Samios, Peter & Jill Schireson, Rob Schlegel, Roni & Richard Schotter, Jane Scovell, Andrew Seligsohn & Martina Anderson, James & Nancy Shalek, Soraya Shalforoosh, Peggy Shinner, Dara-Lyn Shrager, Joan Silber, Emily Sinclair, James Snyder & Krista Fragos, Alice St. Claire-Long, Megan Staffel, Bonnie Stetson, Yerra Sugarman, Dorothy Tapper Goldman, Marjorie & Lew Tesser, Earl Teteak, Parker & Phyllis Towle, Pauline Uchmanowicz, Rosalynde Vas Dias, Connie Voisine, Valerie Wallace, Doris Warriner, Ellen Doré Watson, Martha Webster & Robert Fuentes, Calvin Wei, Bill Wenthe, Allison Benis White, Michelle Whittaker, and Ira Zapin.